Your Life & Times

How To Put A Life Story On Tape—

An Oral History Handbook

By Stephen and Julia Arthur

Genealogical Publishing Co.
• Baltimore •

Published by arrangement with the authors by
Genealogical Publishing Co., Inc.
1001 N. Calvert St., Baltimore, Md. 21202
First printing 1987
Second printing 1990
Third printing 1991
Fourth printing 1994
Fifth printing 1997

Library of Congress Catalogue Card Number 87-80881
International Standard Book Number 0-8063-1194-0
Made in the United States of America

Dear Friend,

Can you imagine what it would be like to actually hear the voice of your great-grandparents speaking to you, telling you of their own lives and times? Your children and grandchildren and great-grandchildren and their grandchildren will have that opportunity, thanks to what you are about to do.

With *Your Life & Times* as a guide, you will be able to record your life experiences on tape by simply answering questions that will lead you, step-by-step, through the precious moments of your life.

When you finish, you will have completed an oral history of your life and times— a treasure for yourself, and a gift of life and love for your family and for future generations.

Pleasant time-travelling!

TABLE OF CONTENTS

Begin by looking through this handbook. See how it is divided into sections and subjects? With each subject there is a thoughtful list of questions to prompt your memories.

Look through each section, question by question. As you do, it is helpful to note a name here, a date or a few words there, as the memories come back to you. You can also begin to assemble photos or other memorabilia to help you remember or describe people or places from the past .

Look at the questions in the Appendix before you begin taping, in order to determine at what point in your narrative you want to answer those questions too.

Another good way to jog your memory is to talk to others who have lived through those times too. You may want to take notes on those conversations, or even to tape other voices to add to your own taped recollections.

These are the reminders you will be using when you begin taping, so be as detailed in your notes as you can. If there is a question you can't answer, mention that you don't have the information to answer the question so your listener will know you didn't overlook the question.

Keep in mind that the more details you can remember and note, the more your story will come alive in the minds of those yet unborn who will listen to your words!

SOURCES OF INSPIRATION
AND RECOLLECTION

✔Notes or taped excerpts from conversations with relatives

✔Notes or taped excerpts of the memories of old friends and neighbors

✔Photograph albums

✔Heirlooms

✔Legal documents

✔Family documents

✔Family Bible

✔Letters and postcards

The Basics

When you see the words "YOU READ", read the statement into the microphone, supplying the information in the blanks. This tells your listener what topic you are going to talk about next.

When you see the words "YOU ANSWER", simply answer the questions into the microphone. It is not necessary to read the question out loud unless you want to.

Some Preliminaries

THE IDENTIFICATION—
On each tape, the first thing you should do is:
(1.) Say your name;
(2.) Say that you are recording Your Life & Times; and
(3.) Say the number of the tape.

For example: "My name is Jane Miller. I am recording the story of my life and times. This is Tape Number Two, Side A."

THE DEDICATION—
On your FIRST tape only, after the Identification, allow the tape to run silently for about one minute. You can use this "blank space" when you have completed your taping to dedicate your work to someone. A suggested form for the Dedication can be found at the end of this handbook.

Now to Begin

YOU WILL NEED a tape recorder and several 60 or 90 minute tapes of good quality. Practice taping your voice with the recorder to make sure everything is working properly.

SET YOURSELF UP in a quiet comfortable place where you can speak without being disturbed. If you are disturbed by a telephone or other loud noise, remember that it's easy to record over any part of the tape you wish.

GATHER around you all the materials you have collected to help you remember the past.

REFRESH your memory before answering each question. Use the "pause" button when you want some time to think of what you will say next.

DON'T RUSH. Speak in a slow careful voice and if you refer to a person or place with a difficult or strange pronunciation, spell it out on tape. You can save a future family historian a lot of trouble by spelling things out.

OFFER THE DATES of events you refer to as often as you can.

CHECK your recording after the first few minutes each time you begin. Run the tape back a bit to make sure it is recording and to ensure you aren't picking up distracting background noises.

LABEL AND NUMBER the tapes as you finish recording. Don't assume you'll remember later, or that your listener will know which tape to play next, when listening to your recollections.

EXPERIMENT with taping the voices of family members and friends; record familar sounds; play a favorite song; read a treasured poem, letter or newspaper clipping; record a family get-together.

HAVE FUN! You are about to record a very special and unique history. Take all the time you want, and savor the precious moments your memories bring to you as you record them for yourself and your loved ones, for all of time to come.

Some Other Ways to Use YOUR LIFE & TIMES

Audio Taping

This book was written to make it easy for anyone to tell his or her Life Story by answering the questions on the the following pages.

The easiest way to create a Life Story is for you to answer the questions about your own life on audio tape. But there are other ways to use *Your Life & Times* too.

Your Life & Times can be used to record the Life Story of other people. You can ask the questions, and record their answers.

If you are a historian, a free-lance writer, a biographer, or someone compiling the story of an entire family, the questions in this book will prove invaluable.

If you are compiling a Memorial of a loved one you can use the questions contained in this book to create a unique recording.

The tapes you record on are easy to copy using either another tape recorder or a commercial dubbing machine to create an inexpensive but priceless gift for family and friends.

Video Taping

The memories you record on audio tape can be used in conjunction with video tapes too.

If you own a video camera and recorder, or if you decide to rent a video outfit for a weekend, you can videotape visual images to complement your audio tape. If you speak of people, places and times from years ago, you may be able to tape closeup images from your photo album.

You can visit and videotape the places you have spoken of, the former homes, schools and places of work. You can videotape interviews with other family members. You can be as creative as you want to create not only a sound recording, but a sound and visual recording which will be a unique treasure for generations yet unborn.

Transcribing

The answers to the questions in *Your Life & Times* don't have to be recorded on tape, however. If you are more comfortable with the written word, simply writing the answers in the order the questions are presented will give you the structure for a chronological life story.

Word processing technology makes it easy and inexpensive to transform your spoken memories into a printed manuscript which can be duplicated and bound into a limited edition.

My Life and Times

=== My Earliest Years ===

YOU READ:

"My full name is _____.

I was born in (place of my birth) _____

on (date of my birth) _____ *at (time of my birth)*

_____ *to (parents' names)* _____

_____."

YOU ANSWER:

1. What number was I among my brothers and sisters?

2. Where did the family live at that time?

3. What are some of my earliest memories?

4. Do I remember any favorite toys, playthings or family pets from my earliest days?

5. Are there any photos of me as a young child? What did I look like?

6. What toys did I play with as a small child?

7. What relatives and family friends were around me during those earliest years?

8. What were my parents doing for a living then?

9. Do I remember any rhymes, stories or games from those earliest years?

10. Can I describe my mother at some typical activity? (sewing, reading stories, coming home from work, etc.)

11. Can I describe my father then, busy at some remembered activity typical of him?

12. Can I describe the place(s) where my family lived during my early years?

13. Can I describe my brothers and sisters at some typical activity during that time of my life?

14. Who were some of my first playmates?

15. How was my health during those early years?

16. Do I have some vivid memories from those years?

17. How have the practices of training young children changed since I was a young child?

18. Can I describe the kinds of clothing we wore at the time, the kinds of transportation we used, or the general surroundings in which we lived at the time?

Starting
School

YOU READ:

"I started school at the age of _____ . "

YOU ANSWER:

1. Where was the first school I attended located and how far was it from my home?

2. What was the school's name?

3. Can I describe what the school looked like?

4. Are there any pictures available from those school days?

5. What can I remember of my first day at school?

6. Were any of my brothers or sisters already in school?

7. Who was the principal and what did he/she look like?

8. Who was my teacher and what did he/she look like?

9. Who were some of my classmates?

10. As I progressed through school, who were some of my favorite teachers?

11. Who were some of my best friends?

12. How did I get along with my schoolmates?

13. Which subjects did I do well in, and which subjects were not my best?

14. Did I discover any special interests, talents or abilities as a student?

15. Did I have to change schools?

16. What did I do after school was over in the afternoon?

17. How did I spend my summers during my early school years?

18. Did I ever get crushes on a schoolmate or a teacher?

19. What stories can I tell of those days?

20. What stories can I tell of my brothers and sisters during that time?

Growing Up

YOU READ:

"Now I'm going to describe what it was like growing up in my family."

YOU ANSWER:

1. What were the general relationships among members of my family while I was growing up?

2. Did I have a strict upbringing?

3. Did my parents emphasize achievement in school?

4. How religious was my family?

5. What rules did I have to abide by?

6. Did I have any special chores or obligations? What about my brothers and sisters?

7. How did I get spending money?

8. What would happen to me when I disobeyed my parents or got into trouble?

9. Did I get into trouble much?

10. What is the worst trouble I can remember getting into as a child or as a teenager?

11. Did my brothers or sisters get into trouble?

12. How did my parents share family responsibilities?

13. Did my parents have an active social life?

14. Can I describe how my parents spent a typical day?

15. What friends or relatives or neighbors were an important part of the family scene?

16. What attitude did my parents hold toward money, possessions and "what the neighbors might think?"

17. What hardships did my parents have to face?

18. What hardships did I or my brothers and sisters have to face?

19. Can I describe a typical day in the life of my brothers and sisters?

20. How did my family celebrate holidays?

21. What family events still stand out in my memory?

22. What wonderful qualities did each of my parents have?

23. What not-so-wonderful qualities did my parents have?

24. What values did my parents try to instill in their children?

25. In what ways am I like either of my parents?

26. In what ways are my brothers and sisters like either of my parents?

(Note: If you didn't go to high school, tell what you did instead, and go to the next group of questions which apply to your situation.)

YOU READ:

"I started high school when I was _____ years old."

YOU ANSWER:

1. What was the name of the school?

2. What did the building and grounds look like?

3. Who was the principal of the school?

4. What teachers do I remember, and why?

5. How well did I do in school?

6. What were my special interests?

7. Did any subjects give me a lot of trouble?

8. Were sports a big part of my life then?

9. What school activities did I participate in?

10. Did I have any after-school jobs?

11. Who were some of my friends during my high school years?

12. Did I have any brothers or sisters going to school with me at the time?

13. How did we entertain ourselves in our free time?

14. What was going on in the world around us then?

15. Did I date anybody, or have any crushes?

16. Did I have an opportunity to drive a vehicle during those days?

17. How did others regard me during those years?

18. What has happened to those people since then?

19. Have any of my classmates gone on to become rich, famous or notorious?

20. What did I plan to do after leaving school?

21. When did I leave school?

22. What did I do after leaving school?

College or Trade School

(Note: If you did not go to college, go on to the next group of questions .)

YOU READ:

"I began college (or trade school) when I was _____ years old."

YOU ANSWER:

1. Why did I decide to go on with school?

2. How did I choose the school I went to?

3. Did the school meet my expectations?

4. Can I describe the place(s) where I lived during these years?

5. How did I pay for my studies?

6. Can I describe a typical day in my life as a student?

7. How did I spend my summers?

8. What was my major field of study?

9. Did I have a favorite professor?

10. Did I have an active social life then?

11. Who were some of my more memorable friends?

12. What did we do for entertainment then?

13. Did I date then?

14. Do I know what has become of some of the people I knew then?

15. What crises did I face during those years?

16. What did I achieve in school?

17. What plans did I have before I left school?

18. How have those plans worked out?

19. Did I graduate? When was that? What was my degree?

20. What did I do afterwards?

(Note: If you went to graduate school, please answer the above questions again for that phase of your life before going on.)

My Father and Mother

YOU READ:

"My Father's/Mother's full name is _____.

He/She was born on _____ *in* _____."

YOU ANSWER:

1. What number was my Father/Mother among his/her brothers and sisters?

2. Who are his/her brothers and sisters, from oldest to youngest?

3. Where did he/she grow up?

4. Does he/she tell any stories from that time?

5. What was his/her childhood like?

6. What kind of upbringing did he/she have?

7. How did he/she get along with the rest of his/her family?

8. What did he/she look like as a young person?

9. Are there any pictures of him/her at those ages?

10. How much education did he/she have?

11. What kind of work has he/she done?

12. What was his/her life like before his/her marriage to my Mother/Father?

13. What early ambitions did he/she have?

14. How have those dreams worked out?

15. Does he/she have any special talents or skills?

16. How can I describe his/her "character?"

17. What have been his/her most difficult times?

18. What have been his/her most important achievements?

19. What else can I think to say about my Father/Mother?

My Aunts and Uncles

YOU READ:

"Now I'll be talking about my AUNTS and UNCLES on my Father/Mother's side."

YOU ANSWER:

1. Who are my Father/Mother's brothers and sisters, from oldest to youngest?

2. When were they born, and where?

3. What can I remember about each of their early years and youth?

4. Do they have any nicknames? How did these come about?

5. Are there any stories I can tell about them as kids?

6. What are they like now as adults, and what do they do?

7. When and to whom did each get married?

8. Who are their children? What can I tell about each of these cousins?

9. Do I see much of my relatives? Where are they living?

10. If any have died, when and how did this happen? Where are they buried?

11. Are there any interesting stories about these aunts, uncles, and cousins?

(Note: Now answer the questions again for aunts and uncles on the other side of the family.)

My Parents Together

YOU READ:

"My PARENTS were married at (place of marriage)

_____

on (date of marriage) _____ *."*

YOU ANSWER:

1. How did my parents meet?

2. When did they meet?

3. Did they have a long courtship?

4. Do they have any stories of the wedding or honeymoon?

5. How old were they when they got married?

6. Where did they first live after the marriage?

7. Were there other family members living nearby?

8. How did the couple adjust to their new in-laws?

9. What stories have I heard of their early years together?

10. What was their early financial situation?

11. How were they earning a living?

12. Can I describe what my Father/Mother looked like at that time?

13. Are there any pictures of them at that time?

14. As a young family, what were their hopes and expectations regarding children?

15. Are my parents still living?

16. What are their circumstances now?

14. If they have died, where and how did this happen?

15. If they have died, where are they buried?

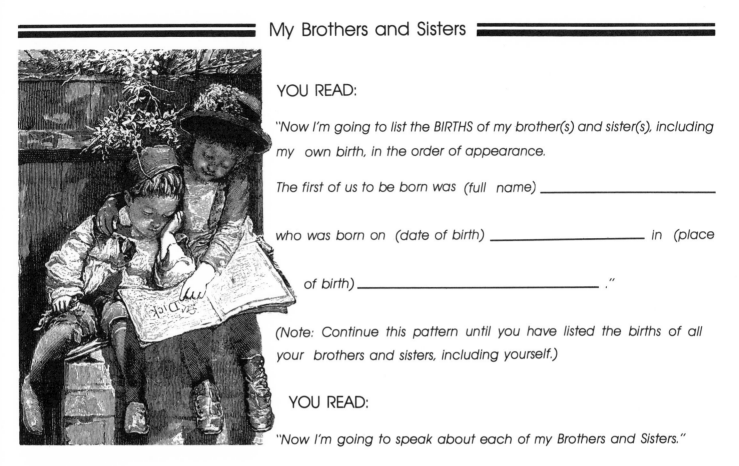

YOU READ:

"Now I'm going to list the BIRTHS of my brother(s) and sister(s), including my own birth, in the order of appearance.

The first of us to be born was (full name) _____

who was born on (date of birth) _____ in (place

of birth) _____ ."

(Note: Continue this pattern until you have listed the births of all your brothers and sisters, including yourself.)

YOU READ:

"Now I'm going to speak about each of my Brothers and Sisters."

YOU ANSWER:

1. Do I know anything about his/her birth?

2. What early memories do I have of him/her?

3. Did he/she have a special family nickname?

4. If so, how did this name come about?

5. What kind of temper did he/she have?

6. How did we get along as children?

7. What sort of relationship did he/she have with the rest of the family?

8. What traits did he/she exhibit at an early age that can still be seen in adulthood?

9. Did he/she show any special talent or ability?

10. What early ambitions did he/she have?

11. How did those ambitions work out in later life?

12. How did he/she do in school?

13. What level of education did he/she achieve?

14. What was he/she like as a teenager?

15. Who were some of his/her friends?

16. When did he/she show an interest in the opposite sex?

17. What memorable family occasions can I recall involving him/her?

18. What did this sibling look like in younger years?

19. Are there any pictures available of him/her as a younger person?

20. What has he/she done since leaving home or school?

21. How does he/she earn a living?

22. Are there any stories I can tell which exemplify the kind of "character" he/she has?

23. Has he/she married?

24. To whom, when and where did this marriage take place?

25. Has he/she divorced?

26. Who are his/her children?

27. What has been the most difficult time for him/her?

28. What have been his/her greatest achievements?

29. Where is he/she living now and what is he/she doing now?

30. If he/she has died, what were the circumstances of death?

31. If he/she has died, where is the place of burial?

32. What else can I think to say about him/her?

(Note: Answer these questions to the best of your ability for each of your brothers and sisters.)

================================ My Spouse ================================

YOU READ:

"I am going to tell you now about my HUSBAND/WIFE, (name of your spouse) _____

who was born in (place of birth) _____ on (date of birth) _____ ."

YOU ANSWER:

1. Who were my spouse's parents?

2. What number was he/she among his/her brothers and sisters?

3. What are the names of my spouse's brothers and sisters?

4. Where did he/she grow up?

5. What did his/her father and mother do for a living?

6. How might my spouse's parents be characterized?

7. What was the atmosphere of the family circle in which my husband/wife grew up?

8. What do I know about his/her early upbringing?

9. How religious was the family?

10. Can I tell any stories I have heard about my spouse's childhood?

11. What kind of schooling has he/she had?

12. What were my spouse's early ambitions?

13. How have these early dreams worked out?

14. What did my spouse do from the time he/she left home, until the time we were married?

Courting Days

YOU READ :

"I first met (your spouse's full or maiden name) _____

at (place you met) _____ on (date

you met) _____ ."

YOU ANSWER:

1. What were the circumstances of that first meeting?

2. What did he/she look like?

3. What did I look like?

4. What was his/her situation in life at the time?

5. What was my life situation at the time?

6. What was his/her impression of me?

7. What was my impression of him/her?

8. How did we become involved?

9. Can I tell some stories of our courting days?

10. What were the circumstances of the proposal?

11. Did either of us have any doubts about getting married?

12. How did our friends and families feel about our relationship?

13. When and where were we married? In what kind of ceremony?

14. Can I give details concerning the wedding and the honeymoon?

═══ Our Marriage ═══

YOU READ :

"I have been married to (name of your spouse) _____

for (how many years?) _____ *as of this date, (today's date)* _____*."*

YOU ANSWER:

1. Had I ever considered any alternative to marriage?

2. Did I have a true idea of what marriage was all about when I got married?

3. What changes did I have to make in my life after getting married?

4. Did we have any problems adjusting to being married when we started out?

5. How did we work out difficulties between ourselves?

6. Where did we first live?

7. Can I describe details of life during that time?

8. Who were some interesting neighbors during that time?

9. Were friends or relatives living nearby?

10. What were we doing to make a living then?

11. What sorts of wages were being paid then?

12. What were the prices of things then?

13. What did we do for entertainment then?

14. Where have we lived since that first home?

15. How has our financial situation changed over the years?

16. What were our thoughts about having children when we first got married?

17. How have those expectations manifested themselves over the years?

18. Name, in order of birth, all of the children resulting from this union.

19. How did my spouse and I share household and child-raising responsiblities?

20. What pets have we had? (in order of appearance).

21. Can I describe a typical day in the life of the family as it was during our child-rearing days?

22. How did we observe special holidays?

23. What hardships have we faced during the course of our marriage, and how were they dealt with?

24. What have been some of the joys and rewards of our marriage?

25. How do we generally resolve our differences? (examples?)

26. Have either of us ever thought of divorce as a solution to any of the problems we faced?

27. What changes have I observed in marriages and in family relationships over the years?

(Note: If you are still married to this spouse, you can go on to the next group of questions now. Otherwise, continue the next two "READS" if they apply to your situation. After, you can answer the questions on MARRIAGE AND FAMILY for each situation in its turn.)

YOU READ:

"That marriage ended in (divorce, annulment, death of spouse, etc.) _____

on (date) _____ ."

YOU ANSWER:

1. What were the circumstances?

2. What have been the long-term effects of the end of this marriage ?

YOU READ:

"My second (third, fourth, etc.) marriage was to (full name of spouse) _____ . We

were married on (date of that marriage) _____ ."

(Note: Now go back and answer the MARRIAGE AND FAMILY questions for any subsequent marriage(s).

YOU READ:

"I'm going to speak about my CHILDREN'S BIRTHS.   My first child who is

named (full name of first-born) _____

was born on (date of his/her birth) _____ in (place of

birth) _____ . My next child, (name of next-born) _____

_____ , was born on (date of birth) _____ in (place of

birth) _____ ." and so on.

(Note: Answer the following questions for each of your children in order of birth.)

YOU READ:

"When (name) _____ was born, we were living in (place at time of

his/her birth) _____ ."

YOU ANSWER:

1. How were we earning a living then?

2. Describe the place we were living then, including the area around the home.

3. Were we financially prepared to have a child?

4. How did our families react to the news of the pregnancy?

5. Was it a difficult pregnancy?

6. What were the exact time and circumstances of the birth?

26

7. How much did the child weigh and what did the child look like at birth?

8. Did the baby experience any problems during early infancy?

9. How was the baby cared for during that time?

10. How quickly did the baby develop?

11. How was the child named?

12. Did the child's brothers or sisters have trouble adjusting to having a new baby in the house?

13. Was the child the particular favorite of any other family member?

14. What character traits did the child show at an early age?

15. How difficult or easy was it to care for this infant?

16. What else can I think to say about this child's first years of life?

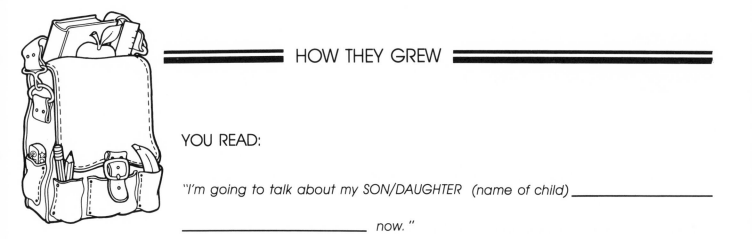

HOW THEY GREW

YOU READ:

"I'm going to talk about my SON/DAUGHTER (name of child) _____

_____ *now."*

YOU ANSWER:

1. Did this baby bear any family resemblances at first?

2. How would I describe his/her temperament as a young child?

3. Were there any other children, relatives, friends or pets in the household at that time?

4. At what age did my child learn to smile, to sit up, to crawl, to walk, to speak, to use a toilet, to count, and to read?

5. What were his/her first words and phrases?

6. What were some favorite pastimes of this child?

7. As this child grew, what characteristics in appearance and behavior developed?

8. What special talents or abilities did this child exhibit?

9. What were some of the family's favorite things to do together as the child was growing up?

10. How was the child's health during those early years?

11. How did this child get along with the others in the family?

12. Did this child have any special chores or responsibilities around the house?

13. How did this child get along with other children outside the family?

14. How did this child adjust to school?

15. What kind of report cards did the child bring home?

16. How did this child typically spend playtime?

17. If this child listened to the radio or watched television, what favorite programs did the child enjoy?

18. Who were some childhood friends of this child?

19. What did this child want to be when grown up?

20. Did this child ever get into scrapes with neighbors or in school?

21. Did the child excel in any activies at school or elsewhere?

22. What schools did the child attend?

23. As the child grew older, did he/she have any after-school jobs?

24. Did the child suffer any physical injuries?

25. Did the child suffer any psychological traumas while growing up?

26. When did this child show an interest in the opposite sex?

27. When did this child begin driving?

28. How did this child do in high school?

29. Did you ever worry about the future of this child?

30. What level of formal education did the child attain?

31. What did this child do after leaving home or school?

32. What has been the fate of this child since then?

33. Who has this child married?

34. Who are his/her children?

35. What is this child's life situation right now?

36. What values or principals have I tried to instill in this child?

37. What have been some of his/her achievements so far?

(Note: Answer these questions for each of your children before continuing.)

DAUGHTER OR SON-IN-LAW

YOU READ:

"I'm speaking now of (name of child) _____ *and*

his/her marriage(s). He/She was married to (name of your child's spouse) _____

on (date of marriage) _____ *."*

YOU ANSWER:

1. How can I characterize this son/daughter-in-law?

2. Where is he or she from originally?

3. What is his/her background?

4. What is his/her education and work life?

5. Who are his/her parents? What are they like and where do they live?

6. How did my child meet this spouse?

7. Can I describe their courtship?

8. What did I think of their decision to marry?

9. When and where was the wedding held? Can I describe the ceremony?

10. How would I describe their life-style?

11. What are the names of the children who resulted from this marriage?

12. Where and when were the children born?

13. If this marriage ended, describe the circumstances as best you can, and how it affected the family.

14. If the marriage ended, how did it affect your child?

15. Were there any subsequent marriages?

(Note: If your child has had more than one marriage, go over the above questions again to mention any subsequent spouses and children resulting from those other relationships.)

My Grandchildren

YOU READ:

"I'm going to speak now of my GRANDCHILDREN, and I'll start with my first one."

YOU ANSWER:

1. Who is my firstborn grandchild?

2. Who are his/her parents?

3. When and where was this grandchild born?

4. Does this child have any family resemblances?

5. How would I characterize this child?

6. What are my first memories of this child?

7. What were my thoughts upon becoming a grandparent?

8. Do I have any stories to tell about this grandchild?

9. What has my role been in this child's life?

10. How old is this grandchild today?

11. Where does this grandchild live today, and what is he/she doing?

12. Why am I proud of this particular grandchild?

13. What do I hope for this grandchild?

14. What else can I think to say about this grandchild?

(Note: Repeat these questions for each of your grandchildren)

Military Service

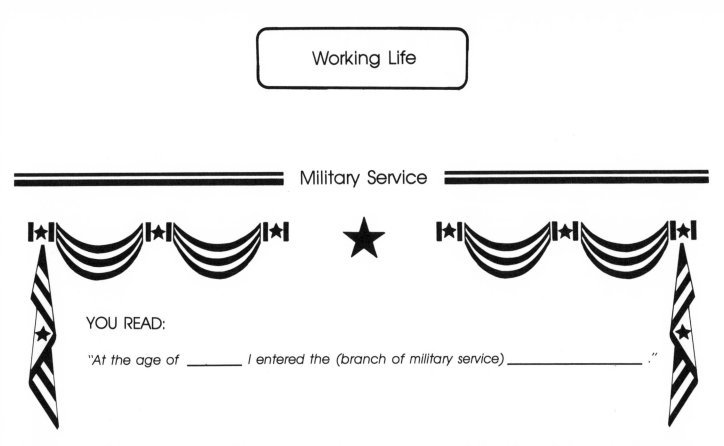

YOU READ:

"At the age of _____ I entered the (branch of military service) _____ ."

(Note: If you did not enter the military, go on to the next set of questions that apply to your situation.)

YOU ANSWER:

1. What was my life situation at the time I entered the service?

2. Did I volunteer or was I drafted?

3. What was the world situation at the time?

4. How did I happen to get into the particular service I found myself in?

5. What was the reaction of my family and friends when I entered the service?

6. How long was my service obligation?

7. Can I remember my service number?

8. Where did I have my basic training?

9. Can I describe the training camp?

33

10. Can I describe some of the people I trained with?

11. What was a typical day like during basic training?

12. What was I trained to do?

13. Where was my first duty assignment?

14. What was it like?

15. Who were some of the people I worked with?

16. What did we do for relaxation?

17. Did I have the opportunity to see foreign lands?

18. Where else did I serve during my military service?

19. If I served during wartime, did I see combat? If so, can I describe some of the situations?

20. What tales can I tell of those days, places and characters?

21. Have I maintained contact with old service friends?

22. Have I availed myself of any veteran's benefits?

23. Do I belong to any veteran's organizations?

24. Would I recommend military service to young people today?

25. What did I do after I left the service?

YOU READ:

"I'm going to speak about my WORK HISTORY, which spans about (number

of years you have worked) _____ *years. During that time, I have*

worked as a (list the jobs you have held over the years) _____

_____ ."

YOU ANSWER:

1. As a child, what did I want to be when I "grew up"?

2. How did I decide upon an occupation or career as I became older?

3. How did I prepare myself for this occupation or career?

4. How old was I when I first began working?

5. Did I work through my school years?

6. Can I describe the wages and working conditions of that first job?

7. What were my subsequent jobs, wages and working conditions as I grew older?

8. What did I do with the money I earned from those jobs?

9. What did I learn about life from those first experiences?

10. What was my first full-time job? What was the wage, and what were the working conditions?

11. Who were some of the memorable people I worked with then?

12. What were some of the stepping stones, or turning points, in my work history?

13. What was going on in the world during my first working years?

14. How did these events affect me in my work?

15. Who were some important people who were instrumental in my progress during my worklife?

16. Did I ever have ambitions of attaining wealth or prominence, or of starting a business of my own? **(Note: See questions on MY BUSINESS).**

17. Can I describe the rest of my work history, job by job, until my most recent one?

18. Have labor unions played a role in my working life?

19. What changes have I observed in the workplace since entering the workforce myself?

20. Do I have any suggestions to offer young people who are in the workforce already, or who are preparing to make their way in the world?

21. If I had the chance to prepare again for a working life, what sort of preparations would I make, and why?

22. What has the word "success" meant to me in the past, and what does it mean to me today?

23. What else can I think to say about my own life's experiences in the workplace?

My Business

YOU ANSWER:

1. What is or was the nature of my business?

2. How did I decide to go into this business? When was this?

3. Can I describe its beginnings?

4. Were there any crises? How did we handle them?

5. Can I give a year by year account of my business's growth and change?

6. What do I see for the future?

7. Do I have any advice to anyone contemplating a business venture?

Retirement Plans

YOU READ:

"I am not yet retired. I plan to work for _____ more years."

(Note: If you are NOT retired, answer these questions. If you ARE retired, go on to the next set of questions.)

YOU ANSWER:

1. When do I plan to retire?

2. What kind of financial arrangements am I making?

3. Am I looking forward to being retired? Why, or why not?

4. What activities will I pursue?

5. How do I anticipate that my daily life will change, and how will it stay the same?

Retirement Days

YOU READ:

"I retired from (company or occupation) _____

(how many) _____ years ago, at the age of _____ ."

YOU ANSWER:

1. What had been the nature of my last job?

2. How long had I been with that company?

3. What kind of send-off did I have?

4. When did I begin planning for my retirement?

5. Did I have a difficult time adjusting to my retirement?

6. Did my spouse have a difficult time adjusting to my retirement?

7. How did I imagine my retirement would be?

8. Were my expectations of retirement fulfilled?

9. What is the nicest thing about being retired?

10. What is the most difficult thing about being retired?

11. Did I miss my work schedule at first?

12. What habits did I have to change?

13. What is my daily schedule like these days?

14. What are some of my future goals?

15. What physical activities do I enjoy?

16. Do I have any advice for a young or middle-aged person who may one day be able to retire?

17. Has my view of the world changed since retiring?

18. If I had my life to live over again, what would I do differently, and what would I leave the same?

19. What else can I think to say about my retirement years?

The following groups of questions are provided for you to answer as you deem fit in the course of your taping. You may wish to incorporate them into your life story, or answer them as separate topics.

Moving Homes

YOU ANSWER:

1. How long had we/I lived at ...(address of your previous home)... before it was decided to move?

2. Why was that move made?

3. What events took place within the walls of that previous home, which made the place memorable?

4. How did we move our belongings?

5. What did the new place look like?

6. What was the address of the new place?

7. How long did we live there?

8. What made it a good place to live? What were some of the drawbacks?

9. What important events took place there?

41

10. Did the neighborhood or area around that place change while we were living there?

11. If we moved again, where was the next move, and why was it made?

(Note: Answer the above questions again for each place where you or   your family has moved.)

━━━━━━━━━━ Vacations ━━━━━━━━━━

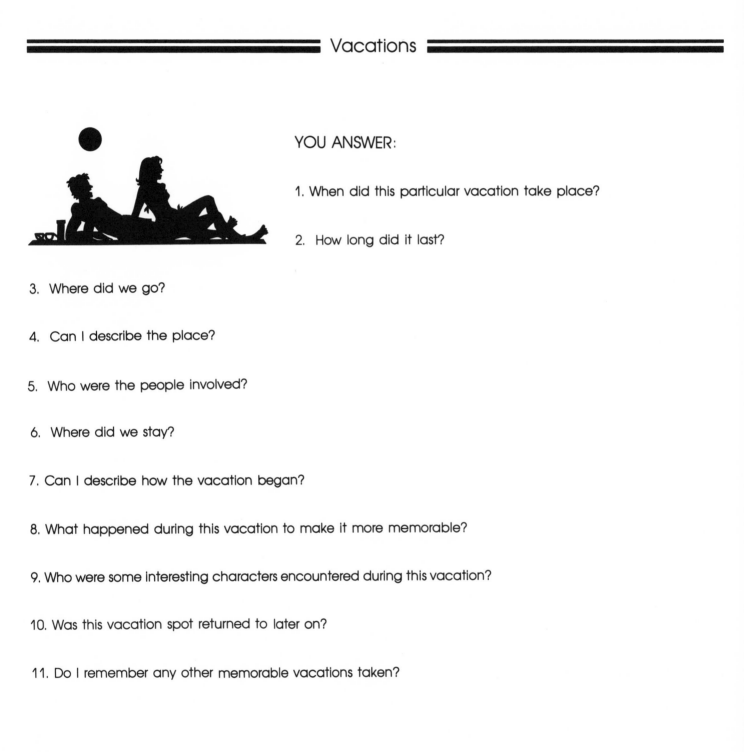

YOU ANSWER:

1. When did this particular vacation take place?

2. How long did it last?

3. Where did we go?

4. Can I describe the place?

5. Who were the people involved?

6. Where did we stay?

7. Can I describe how the vacation began?

8. What happened during this vacation to make it more memorable?

9. Who were some interesting characters encountered during this vacation?

10. Was this vacation spot returned to later on?

11. Do I remember any other memorable vacations taken?

YOU ANSWER:

1. Do I enjoy travelling?

2. If so, why?

3. Where are some of the places I have been so far?

4. Can I describe some particularly memorable journies I have taken?

5. How did this journey take place?

6. How did I travel, and with whom?

7. How long had this trip been planned?

8. Where did I leave from, and where did I arrive?

9. Can I describe what I saw, heard and smelled and my initial impressions of the place?

10. What places did I see along the way?

11. Can I describe some interesting people I met along the way?

12. What adventures did I have during that trip?

13. What impressions do I carry with me from that journey?

14. How long did the trip last, and when did I return?

15. Did I take any other interesting trips later on?

16. What do I think the value of travelling is?

17. How has travel changed during my lifetime?

18. Do I recommend travel to others?

YOU ANSWER:

1. What was the name and nature of this pet?

2. What kind of animal was it?

3. What were the circumstances behind getting this pet?

4. What did it look like when we got it?

5. What were some of this pet's habits or peculiarities?

6. Was this pet a particular favorite of anybody?

7. How long did the pet live?

8. What stories can I tell about this pet?

9. Was that pet replaced with another?

YOU ANSWER:

1. How many cars, trucks, motorcycles, etc. have I owned so far in my life?

2. What was the make, year and color of my first vehicle?

3. What did it cost me to buy?

4. What adventures did I have with it?

5. What did it look like?

6. How old was I when I got it?

7. Why did I get rid of it, and how did I get rid of it?

8. What was my second vehicle?

9. Can I list all the cars, etc. I have owned?

10. Have I ever had an auto accident?

11. If yes, can I describe what happened before, during and after?

12. Have I ever lost a friend or family member in an auto accident?

13. Which of the vehicles I have owned was the best? (describe)

14. Which was the worst, and why?

15. How has the nature of driving changed over the years?

16. What other changes have I seen in transportation over the years?

YOU ANSWER:

1. Do I remember the first telephone my family had?

2. Can I describe it and how it worked?

3. Do I remember the old days of radio?

4. What is the first radio I remember?

5. What programs did I listen to?

6. Did the whole family spend time listening to programs?

7. Do I remember the old days of television?

8. What did my first television set look like?

9. When did my family get its first TV set?

10. What shows did we watch?

11. How does television of today compare with earlier entertainments?

12. What do I forsee for the future in the way of progress in communications?

YOU ANSWER:

1. What favorite foods do I or my family particularly enjoy?

2. Are these foods enjoyed during holidays or are they part of the regular diet?

3. Who has particularly enjoyed these foods in the past?

4. How old is the recipe?

5. Can I describe exactly how it is made, and what the ingredients are?

6. What other foods are served with this dish?

7. What other favorite foods and recipes do I want to pass on to future generations?

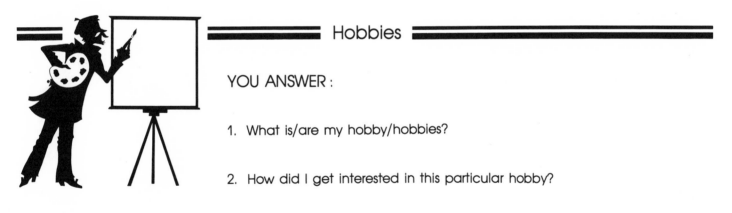

===== Hobbies =====

YOU ANSWER :

1. What is/are my hobby/hobbies?

2. How did I get interested in this particular hobby?

3. How old was I when I began to pursue this interest?

4. Had I considered this hobby before?

5. What value does this hobby have for me?

6. How much time do I spend with it?

7. What are some of my other interests or hobbies?

YOU ANSWER:

1. Has religion been an important part of my life?

2. Was I raised in any particular faith or belief?

3. What are some of my earliest memories of religious ceremonies or practices?

4. Was there a particular event or occurrence which either weakened or strengthened my religious convictions?

5. Who were some important people in my life who helped influence my thoughts on religious matters?

6. Do I belong to a particular church, congregation, temple or other religious group?

7. What role has religion played in my family's development?

8. Has my understanding of religion changed over the years?

Philosophy of Life

YOU ANSWER:

1. Upon what principles have I based my life?

2. What ideas have been important in my life?

3. How did I come to believe as I do?

4. What people have there been who have influenced me in the beliefs I have developed?

5. What advice can I offer to anyone who may be struggling to understand the nature of his or her life?

CONGRATULATIONS!

You have just completed a precious oral history of your life and times.

Now it is time to dedicate your work— perhaps to a loved one, to your family, or to the generations to come who will hear your words long after you are gone.

Remember when you left the first 60 seconds of your first tape blank? Use that blank space now, for the following message or one like it:

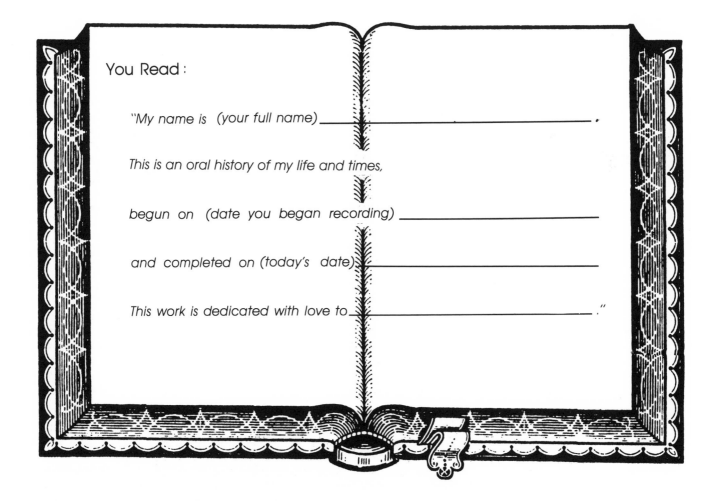

You Read :

"*My name is (your full name)* _____.

This is an oral history of my life and times,

begun on (date you began recording) _____

and completed on (today's date) _____

This work is dedicated with love to _____."

Some Advice for Those Who Want to Search into the Past

Many find that the search for their family history is fascinating enough to become a lifelong hobby. Here are some tips for family historians who want to go beyond the recollections of the living.

HEIRLOOMS & MEMORIES

Begin your research where your family has lived for years, in your hometown.

After you have interviewed your relatives and family friends and have asked for names, dates and places, ask relatives and friends to share letters, photographs, scrapbooks and be sure to read and record all the information you can.

Family heirlooms often have hidden clues in labels, hallmarks, signatures, inscriptions and the like.

GOVERNMENT RECORDS

Courthouses usually hold birth, marriage and death records, along with wills, land and commercial information. Newspapers, too, can be a wonderful source of information about your ancestors.

State censuses and militia records, too, can help you in your search.

Federal records including census schedules, military service pension records, ship passenger arrival information are all available in the National Archives.

GENEALOGICAL SOCIETIES

If possible, join the Genealogical Society in your hometown because they can tell you what source materials are available and how to use them.

BOOKS AND LIBRARIES

There are a number of books available in bookstores and in libraries to help you begin your search for roots.

There are libraries around the U.S. with extensive collections of materials which may help you in your search. The largest repository in the world is the Library of the Church of Jesus Christ of Latter-day Saints, 35 N. West Temple, Salt Lake City, UT 84150. That library has microfilmed original documents from towns all over the world. The library will send microfilms to one of 460 local branch libraries in the U.S. for a small fee.

The Library of Congress, local history and genealogy reading room, 10 First St. S.E., Washington, D.C. 20540 holds published materials which may be a boon, because if someone has already written and published your family history, it will be there.

COURSES

For those who want to dig more deeply, it is recommended that you take a course sponsored by your local genealogical society. If no local courses are available, you can take a home study course offered by the National Genealogical Society, 4527 17th Street N., Arlington VA 22207.

GENEALOGISTS

If you really get stumped, you may want to hire a professional to do the investigative work for you. You can ask around at your own town or county historical society or genealogical library, which can provide you with names of genealogists who work in the area.

Or you can write to the Board for Certification of Genealogists, P.O. Box 19165, Washington, D.C. 20036. For $3 they will send you a list of experts who charge between $20 and $25 an hour for their labors.

GOOD LUCK!